FIFTEEN QUICK AND EASY WAYS TO WRITE A NOVEL

Learn Self-Editing for Fiction Writers

By Susan Summers

Table of Contents

Introduction

Some years ago I read about a new publisher, Oaktara. The two owners, Jeff Nesbit and Ramona Tucker, specialized in Christian fiction and said they were open to new writers and felt major publishers were basically closed to new voices.

I sent them "A Wine Red Silence." They gave a courtesy reply and said they would get back to me in about two weeks with an answer. Two weeks passed and became four. Then I received another polite note from Mr. Nesbit. I asked about my novel. The e-mail that came back basically said, "We liked it. Didn't you get Ramona's e-mail?" No, but it was resent.

Turned out Ramona had written an extensive critique of "A Wine Red Silence," and generally liked it. She did have two or three minor revisions that she requested. But if those were done, she added the company would like to send me a contract.

I readily agreed to the revisions and the book was later published. My one regret is I didn't keep the lengthy critique by Ramona.

But I still remember the excitement and joy I had opening that first e-mail and reading her comments. A real, professional editor who had been in the business for decades had actually read and liked my book. This was a great day!

For a couple of year I also submitted a few science fiction stories to various e-magazine. I still remember the joy when I received an e-mail acceptance notice. (There were a few rejections too.)

This book is a small volume devoted to giving advice to other new writers so they can experience that joy too. Writing can be an extremely frustrating profession. (I often joke that I also like golf so I have TWO exasperating hobbies.)

But it also can be immensely satisfying and rewarding.

This book is exhausting by any means. It's a quick read to give you some advice and counseling about fiction writing. It also include advice on independent publishing and one chapter on what one publishing is looking for in manuscripts and submissions.

I hope it helps any reader improve his writing and gets him or her one step closer from an acceptance from a "Ramona."

Chapter 1:
Plot – Every Novel Should Have One

In Robert Heinlein's short story "Water is for Washing" the main character does not like water.

So Heinlein throws the Pacific Ocean at him.

This is what is known as giving your character a challenge. It also is a great plot.

In this story, Heinlein has done what every writer hopes to achieve. He has immediately hooked the reader as the man fights for his life, desperately desiring to get back to dry land.

This story also shows reveals everything you need to know about plotting. Create a character then throw everything plus the kitchen sink at him.

Heinlein said once – I believe it was Heinlein – that there are two basic plots. "What if?" and "If This Goes One…"

He took his own advice in "Water is for Washing." The underlying premise of the story is "What if I throw the Pacific Ocean at a guy? Better yet, what if I throw the Pacific Ocean at a guy who hates water!"

Probably the most the most heart-surging current plot under the category of "If This Goes On..." is projecting military successes for ISIS. The terrorists take control of the Middle East and even obtain nuclear weapons. Thousands of fanatical Muslims in the West sympathize with ISIS and will support them. The world teeters on the edge of annihilation.

That might get the readers' attention. A novel with that plot would have a good chance of making the best seller list. In today's political climate, the author might be called Islamophobic but he could laugh about that on his next trip to the bank.

There is perhaps one classic plot in all literature. (1) The author introduces a hero (or heroine) who is a generally a nice, likeable man or woman who the reader sympathizes with. (2) Throw the Pacific Ocean or something equivalent at him or her. (3) He or she attempts to deal with the problem, thus engaging the reader's admiration and respect (4) More and more problems confront the main character. While he's trying to resolve the issue, it looks like he's falling deeper and deeper into a hole and it seems there is no hope. It's only a matter of time until he is killed or destroyed. (5) Against all odds, he triumphs. If the author would like to add a bit extra the main character can learn more about himself, life and the human race through his struggles. Or, as is the case with James Bond, he can simply kill the bad guy and live to fight another day.

Now some may object and say this is a formula and is static. I want to be creative, a beginning writer might say.

That's wonderful but every great writer has used this formula. Like mysteries? Tess Gerritsen uses this formula. Science Fiction? Heinlein used it. The classics? Charles Dickens was not unfamiliar with it. Stephen King has used it. John D. MacDonald used it.

There is ample room for creativity in these five points. The late James Clavell was a master at this and he didn't waste time getting his characters into terrible trouble. Neither does Dean Koontz who has sold a couple of zillion novels. Many of them are incredibly good novels. I haven't read all of Koontz'S work but I've read some and I don't think he has ever deviated from this formula.

One reason this formula works is the similarity to real life. Have you read the novel or seen the film "Unbroken?" The hero has the equivalent of the Pacific Ocean thrown at him. In the end, he triumphs, becomes a true hero. That real life character is one of the finest human beings you could ever know and read about.

If courage is, as Hemingway said, grace under pressure, then the pressure you put on your hero will show his courage and his character.

In some genres, characters are great danger but the challenges do not have to be life or death. Amish love stories are huge in the market today. Of course, the man and woman at the center of an Amish love story will probably not be facing life-threatening events. But they will face challenges to their love. If you can make the Amish man and woman believable, likeable characters the reader will be turning pages swiftly to see if they resolve the challenges and marry.

Some authors insist the literary problems show up immediately. In today's fast-paced world where attentions spans are likely less than three seconds, the challenges must get on the page as quickly as possible.

This means if you're writing a science fiction book, have the aliens attack on the first page, or at least the second page. If you're writing a mystery, have the main character discover the dead guy about three paragraphs into the novel. If you're writing a contemporary novel about the existential questions of life, for pete's sake have something happen to your character on the first few pages so the reader won't tune you out and discard your book. The sooner you hook your reader, the better.

If you're a fantastic writer such as the late John D. MacDonald, you don't need action or threats to get the reader hooked. Pick of his mystery "A Deadly Shade of God" and read the first few lines. If you do, it's practically impossible to put the book down.

In my first novel "A Cold and Distant Memory" this is the opening line.

"I thought it would be a routine case until the car doors locked and Agnes turned left when I told her to go right."

I wanted the reader to know he was in the future, where machines drive cars but are supposed to obey the driver. But something has gone wrong... The reader is immediately thrust into action.

I hoped reading the first line would get the reader to read the second, then the third.

To sum up. One, create an exciting plot. Two, get the reader into it as quickly as possible.

It goes without saying you need a believable plot. However, there are always exceptions to the rule. For more than three, possibly four, decades the late Robert Ludlum wrote thrillers that sold millions on a slow day. Many critics looked down their noses at Ludlum's books but he did have a smooth literary style that, obviously, kept people reading. However, his plots, to be blunt, were not exactly airtight. Here is a backcover description of one of his novels that hit the bestseller list "The Gemini Contenders."

"Dead of night. Salonika, Greece. December, 1939. A clandestine order of monks embarks on a desperate mission: to transport a mysterious vault to a hiding place high in the Italian Alps. Its sinister contents, concealed for centuries could rip apart the Christian world."

Of course it could.

On a realistic scale, with 10 being the highest, this comes in at 0.1. Ludlum also has the monks killing anyone who gets in their way. If you happen to know anyone who lives a monastic life, you realize this is a stretch.

Which brings up another issue.

If you are a good writer and are, like Ludlum, writing thrillers you can sell a less than credible plot to the reader if your prose is good, exciting and readable. It's the suspension of belief. But even Ludlum and other professionals can't sell a scene that's illogical.

I'm a great admirer of the late Robert Parker. His "Spenser" novels are first rate. But in one novel, when Spencer and Hawk are investigating a matter, several thugs try to beat them up to get them off the case. Trying to take on Spenser and Hawk is not a good idea unless you have the 82nd Airborne on your side. There is also no reason for the assault. The duo is investigating but has found nothing worthwhile. No clues, no evidence. Nothing. So why try to get them off the case? No reason. In fact, the assault proves to Spencer and Hawk that they shouldn't drop the case. The scene perks up the action in the novel but is dumb.

Irene Hannon is a Christian novelist who also writes mysteries. In one of her books, she does the same thing – a hitman tries to kill her main character although there's no valid reason for the attempted murder. Hannon realizes this and knows it's a stretch. She has the assassin admitting he made a mistake and panicked when he should have kept calm. A nice touch but the scene is still a bit thin. Both scenes were meant to provide a little excitement when the novel might be getting dull. But most readers can see through that.

Don't let it happen in your novels.

Chapter 2:
Writing Groups

Now I want to talk about something rarely mentioned in books about writing but is very valuable and will save you a great deal of money.

Writing groups.

Such groups are very valuable and can give a beginning writer incredibly good advice. You can read all the books on writing by such authors as Dean Koontz, Lawrence Block and Elizabeth George – which would probably be a good idea – but those authors are not in your house to look over your most recent chapter. They have no firsthand knowledge of your contributions to literature.

Writing group members can give you immediately feedback and, most of the time, their critiques are valid. These are individuals who also enjoy writing and may have been scribbling stories or novels for years. A few may have been published, and a few may have any number of insights into the writing process.

Beginning writers often wonder if they should go to writer's conferences or join writing groups. In terms of the latter, yes. In terms of the former, it's a maybe at best. Writer's conferences are expensive and most beginning writers are on a low budget. And, I suspect, some conferences are put together for the speakers, not the writers.

When I worked in Harrisonburg, Virginia as an editorial writer, I attended a well-known writers conference just two states away. (Think I got a cut-rate plan.) It was OK but, honestly, it wasn't worth the money. In Harrisonburg, I also joined a writers' group. The valuable insight I received from the group far exceeded the knowledge received at the conference. And the writer's group was free. And I also made some friends.

(The exception is if you can set up an appointment with an editor of a publishing house at a writer's conference. This could be valuable. If so, go for just that day and save some money.)

Not long ago I contracted with a publishing company to write a cozy mystery series. After I completed the first book, the editor seemed pleased (Well, it was a good novel.). Then the company distributed the novel to a number of "readers." I don't know how many readers they used. I'm assuming it was more than one but less than 10. The feedback was generally complimentary but there were one or two comments that led me to do some minor revisions. Clearly, some of the readers were very perceptive. They obviously liked reading and liked mysteries. They praised the strong points of the novel but also noted a few weaknesses. I think the minor revisions made the novel better.

Then the company hired a Beta Reader. I think she also did a good job. However, she was clearly not a golfer. In the novel I had two characters play a brief game of golf. The Beta Reader did not realize golf has men's and women's tees.

Which bring up another issue. While the critiques are worthwhile, there will be times when Beta Readers and others miss it. As a writer you have to make the determination when a reader gives insight into your work and when their comments seem to be coming from the Twilight Zone. Authors do have blind spots but so do readers.

I don't know how the company hired their "readers" but the readers would easily have been members of a writing group. Their comments on the novel reminded me of the two writing groups I have been in. Excellent advice was given in both cases.

Readers, Beta Readers and writing group members can spot huge logical errors in your novel or short story. Plotting seems to be a weakness in both novels and films these days. If you're successful and are selling thousands of books every month you can get away with bad plotting. (For example in Lee Child's Jack Reacher novels, I've read a couple of scenes that, to me, were simply not credible. Illogical to the extreme. In one scene Reacher gets into trouble because he forgets to take his gun with him. Of course, many other scenes were exciting and realistic. The editors must have noticed the illogic but didn't seek changes. Child is a best selling novelist and can get away with this...to a degree. If it spins out of control, sales may suffer.

While Mr. Child may get away with it, a beginning writer can't. If you haven't built up trust with your readers, they won't give you a suspension of belief. Nor should they have to. If you're writing realistic fiction, your characters should behave in realistic ways.

Chapter 3:
Writing the Blockbuster Novel

The title of this chapter is something of a misnomer because no one really knows how to write a blockbuster novel, although I suspect marketing helps. It is a fact that some very bad books sell millions of copies.

So I won't offend any living writers, let me mention a few dead ones to make a point. It's said we should not speak ill of the dead but, as Harold Bloom pointed out, if we don't, who will?

In my late teens when I was thinking seriously about writing as a career, there were three best selling novelists typewriting their way to the top – Harold Robbins, Irving Wallace and Jacqueline Susann. Critics generally agreed these three writers were awful. Not just bad, but truly, truly awful. Yet their books were listed in single digits on every best selling list in the nation.

How?

To be honest, no one knows.

Writer Harlan Ellison said he was working on the screenplay of Susann's "Valley of the Dolls" before it was even printed and said it was bought onto the Best Seller list. Suzann had contacts in publishing and marketing so I think Ellison's comment was true. It would explain the success of her first book. But people also bought the second and third novels too. What explains that?

And how did Robbins and Wallace get so many readers?

Several years ago, a friend in the newsroom suggested I glance through Robbins' "The Carpetbaggers." He said had read it long ago and remembered how the author had woven various subplots in the novel and tied them together at the climax. As it so happened about two weeks later I saw a copy of "The Carpetbaggers" at a used book store so I picked it up. I think I may have gotten through three chapters before putting it down and probably throwing it away.

I failed to understand why a dozen people, much less tens of thousands, would read the book.

Long ago I skimmed through a few pages of an Irving Wallace novels. It was OK, but I wasn't particularly impressed. Again, I was at a loss to understand why so many copies of his novels were sold.

The answer is, as the theologians say - "It is a mystery."

(An aside. Some years ago Gore Vidal was being interviewed by a magazine writer. During a brief time in the interview he was in a pensive mood and lamented some critics did not like his work. What really irritated him, Vidal said, was often "they speak of me as if I was Irving Wallace." That's a paraphrase but it is very close to the original quote.)

The fact that often bad novels outsell high quality novels is not good news for potential writers. They want to hear if they struggle with plot and prose and create an inventive, original novel that people will buy it. Which is often not the case. However, on the plus side, if you write an incredibly bad novel in the style of Wallace or Susann, perhaps lightening will strike and it will sell millions of copies.

Life, and literary fortunes, are often like that. There are no guarantees in this kind of work.

However, it is also true that if you produce quality work, there is a good chance you will eventually be noticed.

Word-of-mouth is still vital in spreading word about your novel. Perhaps this is even more true in the digital and social media age.

One such novel was "The Shack" by William P. Young. It was fiction but not quite a novel. The daughter of the narrator has been abducted and murdered. Years after her death he is in a shack with God and Jesus and they discuss the questions of life, death and where is God when evil happens.

To the best of my knowledge there was no high energy publicity campaign for "The Shack," but it became a blockbuster. People read it and recommended it to their friends who read it and recommended it to their friends, who read it and... As a result, even seven years after publication, it is still getting numbers on Amazon's Kindle and paperback lists that would turn most writers green with envy.

Now I happen to think Mr. Young's theology is totally wrong, utterly unscriptural and, at times, downright illogical and silly. The novel implies that, at times, losing a job or having cancer can be a good thing. Well, I've lost jobs and also had cancer. Neither of those experiences is pleasant. I based that view both on personal experience and my understanding of scripture.

However, it must be said that the interaction between God, Jesus and the narrator somehow touched readers. Millions of people have read the novel and thousands more are reading it every year. While Young is writing in the Christian genre, many of his readers are secular. In terms of readership, he has transcended the genre.

If I had read "The Shack" before publication I never would have guessed it would become an international best seller. Which shows what I know. My only defense is I don't think many other people guessed the book would become a best seller either.

I'm still not sure what attracted so many people and what continues to attract people to "The Shack." Perhaps it is the unique, but still reverential, treatment of the Lord. Perhaps it's because Mr. Young does address serious theological questions in a conversational style. Perhaps we would all enjoy talking with God in an informal setting and asking him questions about good and evil.

Whatever the reason, the book has been a publishing phenomena. But it is doubtful any writer can reproduce the success of Mr. Young. You just never know which book will take off with the public and which novel people will stay away from in droves.

The best a writer can do is create the best novel possible and then hope for the best.

And use the social media relentlessly.

Chapter 4:
Characterization

Characterization is probably the most difficult subject to write about. While it's possible to boil down different types of action to one basic plot, it's impossible to boil down characterization to a formula.

However, very good characterization can arise from the action in a novel.

For instance, take these scenes.

A young boy knows if his father fibbed a little at a trial he would be rewarded by a good paying job plus bonuses. He would be set for life. But he told the truth. When asked by his son why he didn't back the company offering him financial security, the man replied, somewhat indignantly, "It would have been a lie, son!"

An honest city manager of a good-sized city is threatened with blackmail by some unsavory townspeople. When he attended a state meeting in a bigger city, he spent the night with a woman who was not his wife. The blackmailers say unless he changes his policies they will reveal the truth and claim he even used city funds to pay for his adultery.

His reply: Go ahead. If you want to make it public, go ahead. I regret my mistake but I'm not going to make a bigger mistake by siding with you. But when you go public I will also tell the taxpayers about this little conversation and tell them who tried to blackmail me. We'll let the public decide who is honest and who is not.

An editor of a small newspaper is criticizing several officials who he rightly believes has wasted taxpayer money. The deals they made were not illegal but they were unethical and allowed the officials to enrich themselves at the expense of city taxpayers.

The publisher tells the editor to stop the critical editorials. The officials are advertisers or have friends who advertise with the newspaper. The editor refuses.

He is fired.

Each of these scenes are based on real events. All three show character. All three men, when faced with difficult ethical choices made the right call. If you write these scenes in your novel, these characters come to life. And they come to life by the author showing their dedication and integrity not by simply telling the reader "James Smith was an honest man." You have shown James

Smith in action. He may have, in effect, turned down a huge bribe, called the bluff of blackmailers or stood for principle. But under pressure, they showed grace and courage. If you can write such scenes you have developed a full-fledged, three-dimensional human being who your readers will root for and respect.

These men may or may not share other traits. One may be fat. The other slim. One could be old and another young. One might like baseball and the other two might hate sports. Two might be vivacious extroverts, the third might be an introvert. They may share nothing in common except the solid core of honesty.

Your fictional men and women on your pages do not have to be all that complicated. You do have to go into hundreds of detail about their life, background and whims.

There's a wonderful story Evangelist Joyce Meyer tells about her and husband Dave. She is ruminating that they don't seem to have any "deep" conversations.

Dave, who is polishing a golf club, simply says, 'Honey, this is as deep as I get."

Men will love that answer. Women, perhaps not...

Dave also appears to be a very amiable man with a keen financial sense. He also has to be a man secure in his own skin and not an egoist by any stretch of the imagination. Few men would be comfortable with their wives going on stage and getting all the glory and the fame.

His fiscal abilities are one of his characteristics but the amiable man secure in himself is his character. There's not too many individuals today, men or women, who are that emotionally secure. Your audience might like to read about one. They are not only likeable but they can also inspire a trace of awe.

However, this type of individual will be difficult to sketch out in fiction. He is not a man who will, in the Hollywood phrase, chew up scenery.

There are individuals who have charisma and can suck out the oxygen in a room by walking into it. There are also individuals who are not charismatic at all. But the more you talk with them and the more you interact with them, the more impressed you are with them. The first group are easy to write in fiction. But the second, while harder to get a literary handle on, may make a great and more profound impression on your readers.

You can, if you like, trace out your characters and even make a "profile" of them. List their height, weight, eye color, hair color, tone and pitch of voice, style of speech, any scars, their attitudes about life, hobbies, etc. These can fill out a portrait but don't forget things like hobbies are interchangeable. Whether your main character likes baseball or tennis or soccer or hates all sports, that doesn't reflect his inner core. If you can show his inner core – in three words or three thousand words – you have made your character a complete human being.

There is a tendency, if you have characters who are religious, to make them stick figures. In one mystery I won't name, the author's villain is a born-again Christian. However, his behavior doesn't seem to have changed since he was a sinner. This is not characterization. This is simply a tag put on the man without any thought. It's cheap and basically dishonest. In today's society, this happens too often. If a leftist is writing, all conservatives are dumb and evil. If a conservative is writing, all liberals are equally dumb and even more evil. Many people will buy this, depending on their political views. But such tripe is a disservice to literature and a disservice to honesty.

In fact, a good exercise for all writers is to create a character who is opposite you in terms of politics and faith. Then make him or her a real, three-dimensional, likeable human being.

Back in college, I read some advice from a columnist that said unless you can argue your opponent's position on a political issue – let's pick abortion - and can argue the issue better than your opponent can, you don't have a true understanding of the issue.

The same basic principle is true in fiction.

It may be very difficult but unless a writer can create three dimensional human beings, not stereotypes, of people who disagree with him, perhaps he or she should try another field of endeavor. You may be able to do hack work. But you can never write a high quality novel.

Chapter 5:
Genres

Perhaps the best title in all of fiction is the very unique novel, "Amish Vampires in Space."

No, I didn't make that up.

Darn creative, I'd say.

The author is a Christian and combines Christian fiction, science fiction, Amish tales and vampires in what is a laugh-out-loud title. The book has more than sixty reviews on Amazon and his rating is 4.5. Despite the title, the author plays it straight in the novel. I have a hunch it's a very good read.

It shows a little creativity can go a long way.

The book also somewhat undercuts the theme for this chapter about genres. One of my points was going to be you have to know details about genres before actually penning a novel. But "Amish Vampire in Space" is in a genre of its own.

Back on Earth, each genre tends to have its own rules that you will want to follow. An interesting subculture of the mystery genre is the "Cozy Mystery." Usually, a cozy mystery has a female protagonist who is a business owner but who, alas, keeps getting involved in murders. Murders that she will investigate and solve. There are a few CM novels that do have a male lead character but mostly female businesswomen populate the field. Besides the lead, CM bans graphic violence or sex. The female lead can have a boyfriend but the romance takes a definite back seat to the mystery. If you start writing a CM, it might help to know something about police procedure (a murder does occur in all CM novels) and maybe a bit about businesses. It's perfectly all right and is credible to have the character complain about taxes, but you should give a few details about why she is complaining. To be realistic the character needs to know something about the business she runs and about business and finance in general. You don't have to go into great detail but, when your lead character is not chasing down the killer, it helps to make her sound like a businesswoman.

One item about subgenres. While they can enjoy a sudden explosion of sales – such as the Amish novels today – they may disappear almost as suddenly. Five years from now will people still be reading Amish love tales? Or cozy mysteries? Maybe. But maybe not. You never really know. So you might like to write in two or three genres to keep your options open.

The Mystery Genre has been going strong for a long, long time and will probably continue to do so. Sherlock Holmes may be the most well-known character in fiction worldwide. People simply like mysteries. There are numerous varieties of mystery novels, from the cozy mystery to violent, gritty novels about today's drug wars and cartels.

The best way to find out about mysteries is to read a couple. Tess Gerritsen is a best selling mystery novelist and a very good writer. One of the most positive reviews of her "Silent Girl" on Amazon was written by yours truly. Janet Evanovich writes a very different kind of mystery but is also a skilled writer. A beginning writer might want to read them both and see which style fits him or her.

If you are interested in mysteries, two classic authors you should read are Dashiell Hammett and Raymond Chandler. Two others are Ross MacDonald and John D. MacDonald. The latter two dominated the mystery market in for decades and transformed the field. Their mysteries transcended the genre and were praised by mainstream critics and reviewers. (Which is not always a good thing.) But the two wrote very different types of novels.

MacDonald became a bestselling writer with his iconoclastic detective Travis McGee who, in his own words, was a "slayer of small, savage fish" and had a number of other interesting behaviors too. MacDonald once noted one of the flaws of novelists is pausing to deliver a lecture to readers. This may make the novelist feel good but the trait is often destructive to a novel. MacDonald admitted this was one of his literary flaws.

His character McGee did occasionally deliver off the cuff opinions but MacDonald was such a skilled writer the reader actually enjoyed the literary essays. Most of the time McGee made perfect sense and, even when he didn't you still enjoyed listening to him. But it takes an excellent writer to pull that off. I suggest you don't try it in your first novel.

Ross MacDonald did not have his detective, Lew Archer, deliver any lectures but Archer did solve some of the most complicated, byzantine crimes in the history of fiction. Occasionally, a reader can figure out who the killer is in Agatha Christie's novels. Occasionally. But it was impossible to figure out the villain in Archer novels. But Archer never cheated the reader. After the case was resolved, the conclusion always logical and rational.

The two men also had a different style of writing. Any one interested in writing should read both of them.

As already noted, another genre going strong is Amish novels. In a high-tech age, the Amish have caught on. No one knows how long Amish novels will be popular but they may have the staying power of regular romances, which appear to have infinite staying power. People love romance and a mystery.

But if you do write Amish romances, don't have a character turn on a light. The Amish don't believe in modern conveniences. That's means they don't shower either. That takes a functioning water system, which the Amish don't have. This genre requires some researching so you can get all the details correct.

Chapter 6:
An example of Indie Publishing

Fortunately, I have always found a publisher for my books so I have never been involved in Indie publishing. But an e-mail friend of mine, Denise Rezsonya, went the Indie route with her beautiful "Be the Light," an excellent devotional for the tween set. She was kind enough to describe the process. If you are thinking about publishing independently, reading about her experience, which was positive, should help you and explain the basic details of the process.

When making a decision on a publisher for my first book Be The Light, after a lot of research I decided to self-publish. I made this decision because it allowed me to have full creative rights over my work, it was relatively easy, and it was free.

When trying to decide which company to use for this purpose, I opted for Amazon's publishing house, CreateSpace. I researched several companies but this option appealed to me most because of its association with Amazon. This allowed distribution of my work through many channels by utilizing just one source. It also allowed easy transition to Kindle/electronic format.

The process to publish through CreateSpace is relatively easy. It can be a little confusing the first time through but there is excellent customer service with representatives who are extremely professional and responsive. They also have a dedicated Community section on their website that allows you to research help topics.

The first step in publishing via CreateSpace is to set up an account at https://www.createspace.com. After the account is created, you are assigned a Member ID number. Following that, you go to your Dashboard Page and add your publication by clicking on "Add New Title."

CreateSpace guides you through the process step by step to upload your book content. If you encounter any issues during this part of the process, you are notified with an icon stating "Action Required." The content needs to be uploaded in the correct size format for the book you select and as a .pdf file. You submit cover art separate from the internal book content.

After your book is loaded into CreateSpace, you select distribution channels and pricing. CreateSpace helps you set the retail price of your book depending on the percentage of royalties you wish to receive. Following this, you are given the option to create a Kindle/electronic version of your work.

Formatting for the electronic version can be tricky but you can view it to see if it's the way you want it, and can always resubmit as often as you need to in order to get the format exactly as you want it. For an electronic publication, if your book contains a Table of Contents, it's important to be sure your TOC is in built into your document using the actual TOC feature in your word processing software, to ensure correct updating and to allow hyperlinks from the TOC to the corresponding entry in the book.

After you have gone through these steps and feel your book is the way that you want it, you submit it and within 24-48 hours it will go live. It will get sent through the distribution channels you selected and will be set up in electronic version if you opt for that. You will receive email notification when your book goes live.

Following publication of your work, you can log into CreateSpace any time you have questions. As mentioned earlier, their customer service is very professional and responsive.

They also offer a multitude of free resources and advice for writers including information to assist you in marketing your work.

During this process, you are not charged unless you opt for something within CreateSpace that costs money. You can access your account at any time to check on sales and to see royalty reports. Books are only printed when they are ordered so you do not need to carry stock unless you want to. You do have the option to purchase your books at your cost and have them sent to you.

For libraries and retail organizations wishing to re-sell your book, they do receive discounts to order directly through CreateSpace. They need to have you set them up as a reseller so that they can receive their discount. They are assigned a Member ID and can log in and place orders to dropship directly to them whenever they need to. You can also set up your own promotion codes through CreateSpace should you desire.

Overall, the process to publish in this manner has been extremely positive. The biggest drawback is that you are your own writing, sales, and marketing team unless you can afford to pay a company to do this. It can be extremely time consuming to market the book, which is a benefit some publishing houses offer as part of their service.

For writers who are computer software savvy and can't afford to go through a publisher, Indie publishing with CreateSpace is an avenue worth exploring.

Chapter 7:
Dialogue

"Excuse me, sir, but while we appreciate your rendition of 'Tumbling Tumbleweeds" isn't it time for class to start?"

Oh, yes, it is. Thank you, Diane. Today we will talk about dialogue. In the history of literature there is probably only one author who was able to write dialogue as it sounds in real life – George V. Higgins, the chronicler of Boston lawyers and criminals. If you want to learn how to write dialogue I suggest picking up a few of his books. His characters do sound like real, rugged and often ungrammatical human beings. Higgins was a U.S. attorney and often dealt with the aforementioned ungrammatical human beings. He had both an ear for language and the ability to transfer it to the page. Regardless of the plots, you could read his novels for the dialogue alone.

"Wait a minute, sir. If only Mr. Higgins was able to capture dialogue with authenticity, what do other writers do?"

They write dialogue that sounds realistic to the reader. When two people are talking they will have any number of pauses, stops-and-starts, or choked off phrases in their conversation.

Humans don't talk in the cadence or diction of fictional men and women.

"And, on rare occasions, break into song."

Yes, especially those folks who like "Tumbling Tumbleweeds." All of you are exceptionally talented and I have no doubt you will be publishing novels soon. But probably no one in this class and a microscopic .01 percent of writers can duplicate what George V. Higgins has done with dialogue. It immediately seizes your attention although there are few artful phrases or eloquent statements. The dialogue is so pure and refreshing, the reader is amazed. Because the dialogue is amazing, it keeps the reader hooked, before long, they are also hooked by the plot. As a result, Mr. Higgins wrote any number of best sellers. I don't know his place in literary history but he will always be famous for his dialogue.

"Er, sir, if you don't think we can match Mr. Higgins' in dialogue..."

"That's not really meant as a criticism, Diane. I haven't found anyone who could match Higgins.

"So how do we produce dialogue that sound realistic but isn't?

First, all of us should have something of an ear for dialogue. After all we listen to other people all day long. If one of your characters says something that's unnatural to your ear, then delete it. Two, don't add anything to it. Just write "he said." Not "He insisted," or "he asserted," or "he mouthed." Also, don't describe the dialogue you have just written as "he asserted lamely." New writers tend to do this but it doesn't improve their novel. Dean Koontz wrote once that he only uses "said" in dialogue. It's an ironclad rule with him. I would disagree slightly. I think on rare occasions you can use a different word but don't do it too frequently. You can also, on even rarer occasionally, describe the dialogue. There may well be a place in your novel where "Ferner said the words very carefully, emphasizing every syllable." In some novels and in some situations that might fit. But, as I said, don't get carried away with it.

Dialogue can also help you shape the characters of your fictional creations. It would help if you can have your main characters sound a bit different without using slang or accents.

Long ago, when I was devouring science fiction books, an excellent SF writer made this mistake. His novel was nominated for a Nebula Award, an award given by SF writers for the best novel of the year. He didn't win, possibly because most people in his novel sounded basically the same. Even though his characters came from different backgrounds, they sounded remarkable alike with, if I recall, an odd cadence that they all shared. That's a bad mistake from a very good writer.

In Robert Parker novels, Spencer and Hawk are good friends but the reader can always tell who's talking. Hawk has a distinctive sound, as does Spencer. In John D. MacDonald's novels, Travis McGee has a good friend Meyer and they often discuss various topics. The dialogue sounds realistic, and their dialogue helps define their personalities. But the reader can tell who is speaking because both men sound distinctive in their own way.

Sir, you're singing again.

Oops, sorry. Anyway, since I mentioned those two authors this might be a good time to say that if you are hoping to write a continuing character in a novel, such as a private detective, it might be helpful to give him a sidekick or best friend. MacDonald is an extraordinary writer but he introduced Meyer after about five books into the McGee series. I guess he figured he needed a counterpart to McGee. I think the novels are better with Meyer in them. Spencer introduced Hawk around book three, at first as a villain. Parker must have immediately recognized how good a character Hawk was because he's in most of the other Spenser novels. The books are better with Hawk in them and one reason they are better is Hawk's snappy and distinct dialogue. He matches one liners with Spencer."

After all, Sherlock Holmes had Watson. The Lone Ranger had Tonto. In fiction it's worthwhile to have your main character have a good friend so they can banter with each other and use all that very good dialogue you will write.

Chapter 8:
Outline

Yes, we all want to write soaring prose in the great American novel. But first a writer needs to create a decent plot and here is where an outline comes in.

Some writers say an outline is absolutely necessary before you sit down at the computer and start writing. The reason for this is simple – an author has to know where his novel is going. If not, your attempt at the Great American novel can descend into literary chaos.

An Outline, those authors point out, is akin to a road map. If you have never traveled from, say, Florida to Manassas, Virginia, you need a road map or you will get lost on the way and end up in Tennessee or even Utah. A road map keeps you on the road to your destination. If you follow it, you don't get on back roads or wind up in the ditch.

This is very true. I think it's advisable to have a generic outline of where your novel is going. It can be revised or modified but negotiating a novel is more tricky than driving from Florida to Virginia. A thousand things can trick you up. You need a general destination and few specific travel points along the way.

Having said that, I must admit I am one of those writers who have never been able to outline a novel.

This is not to be taken as a virtue.

For some reason, maybe some type of mental block, I don't seem to have the ability to outline a novel. Some people don't like closed in places. Some people don't like wide open spaces. Some people hate heights. Some recoil at spiders. And some don't seem to be able to do outlines.

Back when I was writing my first novel "A Cold and Distant Memories," typewriters were still used. I remember typing a page and a half then yanking the page from the typewriter, and crumpling it up. Both pages went into the wastebasket. The first line of the novel came to me and I started again, this time not stopping.

My last novel "Last Stand at Lighthouse Point," was crafted the same way. No outline. When I began I knew what the opening chapter would be about and a vague sense of what the last chapter would be, but not much in between. I went from chapter to chapter, usually determining what my next chapter would be after I finished the current chapter.

All in all, I think it worked out pretty well.

But for all of us writers who don't outline, the computer has been a tremendous plus. I did eliminate about 10,000 words in "Last Stand" before submitting it to a publisher. The novel on computer made that a lot easier. You just deleted lines and paragraphs and pages. You can also go back into the novel and add/delete/modify without problems. Back in the days of typewriters you might have to rewrite any number of pages if you went back 10 chapters to change something.

Having said that, it's still preferable to create a generic outline before you write the first word of your novel. You don't get writer's block when you have an outline. You know what your next chapter will be about. You've already have the outline of the chapter in writing. All you have to do is flesh it out. When I was writing "Lighthouse" sometimes I didn't know where the next chapter was going. That's not a problem when you outline.

But your generic outline doesn't have to be totally rigid. It can be changed as you go along. But it's there if you need it.

Some writers will and have said, "How can my readers know what my characters are going to do when even I don't know." Or you might hear a statement like, "The characters took over my novel and I just went with them."

Another novelist might say, "No, they didn't. You're just a sloppy writer and your plots show it."

There are two very distinct views of this. Some writers go with the first method. Others do not. I guessing Dean Koontz never had his characters take over a novel in his literary life.

But I don't think you can be absolute in this. So help me, I am going to try to outline my next novel. I think there are definitely more plusses than minuses when you outline, along as you have a bit of flexibility.

And if you discover you are one of the writers with a mental block about outlining, drop me an e-mail and say hello.

It would be nice to know I'm not the only guy with that problem.

Chapter 9:
Thrillers – In Praise of Alistair MacLean

Writers of good, exciting thrillers and even some writers of mediocre thrillers sell millions of novels every year. The reason is simple. The heroes of their novels get hit with almost every bad thing imaginable and face the challenges with skill, courage, wit and ingenuity. They cheat death and walk away laughing. The plots are often ingenious and the action leave readers on the edge of their seats or staying up until 3 a.m. in the morning to finish the book. While a few elite critics look down their literary noses at this genre, any novelist who can keep his audience reading far into the night and into the early morning deserve some respect.

Which brings us to the late Alistair MacLean.

It is impossible to state with any authority that this author or that author was THE best thriller writer but MacLean would certainly be in the top five. And probably number one.

I was first introduced to MacLean in the seventh grade. Students in my class would give oral book reports, walking to the front of the class, stand behind a lectern and deliver their opinions. One student read MacLean's "Night Without End" and praised it. He was so enthusiastic about the book I decided to find it in the library and read it.

I did and never stopped reading MacLean until he passed away.

In "Night Without End" a plane crashes near a remote scientific research station in the Arctic. Ten people survive. Dr. Mason, one of the scientists, tries to escort them to safety in the bitter Arctic cold that can kill almost instantly if a person doesn't have proper protective gear. Mason discovers the pilot was murdered and that there is a killer among the ten passengers. Thus begins a deadly journey.

MacLean is comfortable writing about Arctic climates. His writing is so precise that, even if you're reading "NWE" in July in Florida while sitting in the sun, you'd be tempted to go inside and put on a jacket. In Maclean thrillers there is often more than one thing trying to kill the characters. There are always human killers around and the weather is often deadly too.

I recently started re-reading "Night Without End" and I was just as impressed with it today as I was long years ago in that 7th grade classroom.

If you want to study thrillers, or study good writing, pick up a few books by Mr. MacLean. You will learn a great deal about every item that produces a good novel – plotting, dialogue, characterization, pace, descriptive writing, action writing, and many other things. You will also learn how to write about heroes. Dr. Mason is not a professional solider or agent, as many of MacLean main characters are but you are quickly impressed with him. Villains are easy to sketch. Heroes are not. But Maclean makes you believe in every one of his rugged, individualist characters. His books will also convince you to stay way the heck away from the Arctic because it is really, really cold up there.

Many of his novels have been translated to the screen and, of course, Hollywood screwed up a couple of them. The film "The Guns of Nararone' departs from the novel but doesn't improve the story. Hollywood totally messed up "Ice Station Zebra," another very good Maclean novel that, at times, doesn't make a whole lot of sense on the screen. The film changes the ending, much to the detriment of the story, and adds a traitor on the crew, which is not in the book. The book is much better. Never rewrite Alistair MacLean. It won't work out.

The one film Hollywood did not mess up was "Breakheart Pass." The reason is because MacLean also wrote the screenplay. If you haven't seen the film or read the book, it is the only time MacLean ventured into the American West circa 1875 for a story.

A train full of soldiers plus civilian officials ish heading to relieve a frontier fort. Also on the train is a Marshall who is taking a dangerous prisoner to the fort. As usual, people start dying. MacLean uses this book to turn some of his plots on their head and it works brilliantly.

There is a cautionary note in MacLean's literary career. His later novels showed a decline and were not nearly the quality of his earlier work. Sometimes this happens with a writer as he ages. The quality of his work diminishes. Sadly, it happened with MacLean. I've read reports that he struggled with alcoholism and perhaps liquor undercut his talent. It wouldn't be the first time the bottle hindered an author's career.

This is incredibly sad because, when he was at his best, he was head and shoulders and chest and torso above any other action writer.

I remember reading one of Maclean's novels about the time I also read one of Donald

Hamilton's Matt Helm books. (Helm was an American James Bond type agent.) Both were writing in the same genre. But in terms of technical knowledge, scientific experience, plotting, pace, and sheer writing ability, MacLean was vastly superior. I'm not putting down the late Mr. Hamilton, because Maclean was vastly superior to any other thriller writer. It's just a reminder of the stark literary distinction between an excellent writer and an average one. (Mr. Hamilton placed many of his Matt Helm books on the best seller list, even if he was only an average writer. Which should give all of us hope.)

There's one other lesson about MacLean's body of work. Many writers hope to write a novel or novel that is remembered after they have passed on. To do this they seek to write the "Great American Novel." That may be a great mistake. Many critical acclaimed novels of fifty or a hundred years ago are unread today, and should be.

However, such writers as Hammett, Chandler, and John D. MacDonald are still read. And Alistair MacLean is still read. And will be, I'm guessing, until the end of literary time.

Chapter 10:
Science Fiction and Literary Politics

As I write this, there is literary internecine warfare being fought in the science fiction genre. Literary feuds are common in the writing world and can often be amusing to the outsider. The beginning writer might say 'Why should I be concerned about a fight in some obscure genre. Will it affect my writing and sales?"

Yes, it could. The fight is also reflective of a larger philosophical/political conflict in society.

The conflict in SF is between the more traditional writers and what might be termed "political correctness' writers. In slang, it is "blue" writers against "pink" writers. Pink being the political correctness writers. These are generic terms and, as such, not incredibly precise but that can't be helped.

The Nebula Awards, the awards given by science fiction writers for the best SF or Fantasy were started in 1965. The winners were:

Novel – Dune by Frank Herbert

Novella – tie – He Who Shapes by Roger Zelazny

Novella – tie – The Saliva Tree by Brian Aldiss

Novelette – The Doors of his Face, the Lamps of his Mouth – Roger Zelazny

Short Short – Repent Harlequin! Said the Ticktock Man = Harlan Ellison

These are all first-rate, triple-A stories. "Dune" is considered by many to be the finest science fiction book ever published. Ellison's "Repent Harlequin!" is also an exceptional story from an immensely talented writer. This Nebula would be the first of many for him. Zelazny and Aldiss are also tremendously gifted writers and were/are among the finest in the field. If you ever want to read some high quality fiction, just read any one of these stories or the novel Dune, if you haven't already.

The winners of the last Nebula Awards are, shall we say, not as well-known as these four writers. The stories that won the 2014 awards - critics would say – are no where near the quality of the 1965 winners.

The 1965 winners were masters of their craft and believed in such things as plot, characters, theme, etc. The more recent winners...perhaps not so much. Critics charge that today politics, instead of good writing, is the prime reason for some stories and books being nominated and winning awards and, indeed, is the primary reason some books get accepted for publication and some do not. This is certainly true to a degree and perhaps a major degree. At one time I read a great deal of science fiction and I have, to a degree, drifted away. I still enjoy the genre sbutI am not familiar with all the details of this major literary battle in the field.

And it is true that editors always favored particular types of stories. When John Campbell was editor of Astounding (later Analog Science Fiction and Fact) he preferred certain types of stories, but he also demanded literary quality. And Campbell was instrumental in getting the best out of his writers. Critics of the pink movement in SF today say that politics triumphs quality in today's science fiction.

So why is all this SF infighting important?

Well, if you want to sell a SF story or a novel, you need to be aware of what type of editor you are dealing with. If you're searching for a magazine to buy your story, you need to know what philosophy the magazine adheres too.

I think John C. Wright is one of the finest SF writers in the genre. In fact, I think he is one of the best SF writers the field has ever produced. If nominated for awards I doubt he would win, although his story or novel would probably be the best.

Why?

His conservative politics and his devout Catholic faith have antagonized many of the Nebula voters. Their views on politics and faith are totally opposite Mr. Wright's. They also may be a bit envious that they can't write as well as he can.

(Update – As it turns out the Huge Award nominations came out about a week after I wrote previous paragraph. Mr. Wright has been nominated for several awards. We will see if he wins.)

But the point is if you want to write SF, you better know the views of the magazine and the editors you are sending stories too. If not, you are wasting your time.

I think this holds true, to a degree, to other genres. If you have a good novel but the editor holds different political views than your main character or objects to whatever in your novel, due to his political, not literary views, you could be in big trouble. This is minefield for writers that was not present, say, twenty or thirty years ago, or at least not present to the degree it is now.

You need to be aware of it.

Lawrence Block, a very good mystery writer, noted once that when he was young he read a great deal of science fiction and enjoyed the genre. So naturally when he started writing he tried writing science fiction. And found he couldn't.

For whatever reason, he could not pen a science fiction tale. His abilities just didn't stretch into the SF genre.

It was wise of Mr. Block to recognize that and stop trying to write SF. Other writers may not be able to write mysteries, or Amish romances or thrillers. If you can't, then quit. Sometimes if at first you don't succeed, you should give up.

There are some signs that the science fiction genre is declining, sales have been down the past couple of years. And the blue SF writers have been saying the pink groups are destroying the field. I had no literary affection for pink SF but the readers will have the ultimate decision. I tend to think the blue material is superior but I might have a blind spot. But sales are impervious to opinions and views. The hard number of sales or non-sales may be the determining factor here. I don't see a great market for pink SF. It is the MSNBC of science fiction and the ratings of MSNBC, as I write, are in the basement. This is not to say a Pink writer couldn't produce a high quality novel. He or she might.

And if you are a pink SF writer and want to produce that high quality novel, there are magazines and editors in the field who will be receptive to you.

Here's a comment by blogger Max Florschutz that sums up the SF dilemma.

"I remember years ago, when I was still in high-school, I used to buy a yearly collection of "best of" science fiction and fantasy stories. And I really looked forward to it … right up until I didn't. Year by year, my interest waned. Not because I stopped reading or enjoying science-fiction or fantasy, but because a lot of the stories included in the "best of" collection simply stopped being stories that I wanted to read. They started to become soapboxes. Character and plot dropped away to secondary importance (if appearing at all) in lieu of social commentary. So I stopped reading."

If long-time readers stop reading and if the genre stops attracting new readers, it will simply fade away.

Chapter 11:
Interlude – Read John Updike, Robert Silverberg and John C. Wright

As noted previously, any person who thinks he or she wants to become a writer and is scribbling down stories or is several chapters into a novel, has to be a reader too. It is not an option. It is mandatory. You learn by reading. You learn style, pace, plotting, dialogue, characterization, etc.

But with one exception, you should not read bad writers. The one exception is – and I've forgotten which author first gave this advice – is if you are in a writing slump. If nothing seems to be going well, if you think the plot is silly and your characters weak and your writing sticks and you're thinking of giving up the literary dreams and going into investment banking...

Then, as therapy, pick up a novel by an extremely bad writer and read a chapter. You should be over come by the feeling of "This is awful. My prose is much better than this garbage!"

That should be enough to get you back to the computer.

One of the names that should be at the top of your reading list is John Updike. More than one critic – and perhaps all of them – have noted his remarkable, flowing prose. It rolls out of his computer the way a refreshing brook rolls down a mountain.

A while back John Foster Wallace wrote a devastating and, at times amusing, review of Updike's "Toward the End of Time." To say the least, he didn't like it. But this sentence is also in the review, "I've continued to read Mr. Updike's novels and to admire the sheer gorgeousness of his descriptive prose."

Probably Updike's writing has never been described better than "the sheer gorgeousness of his descriptive prose."

That line also shows why all potential writers should read Updike, whether or not you think the novel is any good – but it probably will be – read Updike for his prose and learn from him.

Robert Silverberg is most well known for his science fiction work and he has won multiple Nebula Awards, Hugo Awards and every other type of award there is. A few critics have compared him to Updike in terms of prose. He is a magnificent stylist and tells incredibly tales.

One of my favorites is "The Masks of Time." I have reread it a few times to admire Silverberg's prose as well as the plot. The book was written in the late sixties and takes place in 1999 but, even though you know Silverberg's 1999 never happened, you are still enthralled with the novel. "Dying Inside" is another classic by Silverberg. Pick up a book of his short stories – there may be a dozen or more – to learn how to shape and craft shorter fiction. Silverberg was incredibly prolific but the speed of production never seemed to undercut quality when he got serious about writing.

There was a time in his career where, one critic said, he wrote stories that seemed to appeal only to John W. Campbell (then editor of Analog) and no one else. It is true early in his career Silverberg was writing to put food on the table and for other financial reasons. (Don't be snobbish. If you can sell your work, there is nothing wrong with writing for money. Everyone needs money and writing is a legitimate profession.)

But around the mid-1960's, Silverberg was making good money and began writing more serious stories and novels, which may have surprised some of his earlier critics. He became one of the finest authors in the history of the genre.

Silverberg has also published two books of his columns, which he wrote for a science fiction magazine. Usually, the musings of writers, movie actors, political activists can be safely ignored. But Silverberg has a wide-ranging intelligence and is extremely perceptive on almost every subject he writes about. He also has some valuable information for writers when he discusses writing.

A second SF writer I would recommend is John C. Wright, relatively new to the field, at least in comparison to Silverberg who sold his first story back in the 1950s. There are not enough superlative adjective in the English language to describe Mr. Wright's novels. They are simply brilliant. Pick up any one of his works and you will be blown away by his intellect and his prose. One of the many five-star reviews he has on Amazon is mine. He also is a remarkable essayist.

I have already mentioned some writers and I will note a few of them again.

Millions of readers and a high number of writers developed the John D. MacDonald hobby when he was alive and writing his Travis McGee books. It's still a good habit to have. He called one of his McGee books, "Dress Her in Indigo" a "failure." But even a failure by MacDonald would have been a success for most other writers. Even if he felt "Indigo" was not up to his high standards, most of her books were. He used colors in the title of the McGee books and a few of the finest her "A Deadly Shade of God," "Pale Gray for Guilt," "The Girl in the Plain Brown Wrapper," "The Quick Red Fox" and "The Lonely Silver Rain."

You can safely ignore the last few books written by Alistair MacLean but, in his prime, no one would write a better action/adventure novel. You can't go wrong with "Night Without End," "Ice Station Zebra," "Where Eagles Dare," or "Breakheart Pass."

As for techno-thrillers, the late Tom Clancy practically invented the field. Some writers, frankly, are incredibly stupid when discussing anything besides their own work. But Clancy became proficient on military matters and weaponry. Which is why all the military equipment in his novel works just the way he says it does.

It's said Clancy received a boost when it became known that President Ronald Reagan had read "The Hunt for Red October." Reagan couldn't have boosted a better writer. If he gave us Tom Clancy, it's another plus for his presidency.

Chapter 12:
Heroes...and a villain or Two

In a mystery novel soon to be published a private detective is walking into a bar to question a suspect when he sees a man mistreating a woman. He steps in and knocks the guy flat. This doesn't make the suspect, the owner of the bar, happy. When the detective is finished and preparing to leave, the suspect tells him he should exit the region.

"There are no white knights in this county," he growls.

"Sure there are. You're just not one of them," the detective says.

Too many people today, like the bar owner, project their own flaws onto everyone else and onto society. Because of his case, the detective has researched the history of the county and discovered they were a few white knights, men and women who sacrificed for the good of their fellow citizens. He's investigating the murder of one of them. That's a risk white knights sometimes take.

Our culture is a bit uneasy about heroes now. At one time that was not the case. Today often heroes need to be flawed or carry some dark secret with them. Or they must regret of even maybe feel a slight revulsion at what they've done, even though the actions were done in a just cause.

The culture today – meaning Hollywood and publishers – often want a type of moral equivalence between the heroic characters and the villains.

To me, this is nonsense and moral imbecility.

There are a number of soldiers, men and women, who have volunteered to fight with the Kurds against ISIS in today's bloody Middle East. They are risking their lives, and their fortunes to help the besieged Kurds, Christians and other minorities from blood-lusting savages. And probably we will never know their names. But those men and women are some of the most courageous and admirable people on the face of the Earth.

And there is no moral equivalence between them and the ISIS butchers.

Their actions also prove there are real heroes in the world today, so don't be shy about populating your books with heroic characters. Even if society is too embarrassed to recognize them, those heroes make very good characters.

Besides most heroes, if you reflect back, are rather likeable human beings. You like to be in their company.

Your hero doesn't have to be a Lancelot but he does have to know right from wrong. It helps your novel if he is courageous, with dashes of virtue and competence. Likeability doesn't hurt either. He doesn't have to be perfect. He might drink a bit too much or he might be a loner who actually doesn't like people all that much. He (or she) possesses the qualities each of us hope we possess. While an individual might fall short often, the hero rarely does. And when he does he makes up for it somehow.

Atticus Finch, the attorney hero in To Kill a Mockingbird is the image of a virtuous character. He stands up for justice and what is right. Gregory Peck plays him as a low-key man, almost an introvert. So Peck doesn't get flamboyant speeches nor does he chew up the scenery in the film. But his actions reflect what type of a man he is.

Do you want your writing to influence people and be remembered? Any number of lawyers have mentioned "To Kill a Mockingbird" and Atticus Finch as the reason they entered the legal profession.

They wanted to be heroes or at least men who fought for justice, which is not a bad ideal.

Villains are easier to write. They have few, if any, restraints. For your villain, all that people need to know is he has gone over to the dark side. You can probably sketch a villain in a half page. But an Atticus Finch will take pages and pages because you are filling out his personality.

But if you're good at developing a hero and write a good novel, fifty years from now, some man will say, "Yes, I read about Bill Smith in 'Thunder at Bay Beach" and I wanted to follow in his footsteps."

That's a great compliment to a writer.

Chapter 13:
More About Heroes, and Louis L'Amour

Because heroes are so important to a novel (yes, there are some anti-heroes but that's another book) let's spend a few more paragraphs on them. No writer can draw a tough, laconic, stoic hero better than L'Amour in his stories of the American West. Here is a man who lived what he wrote.

No everyone, of course, is a L'Amour fan. Some time ago an elitist, snooty author said she wished every L'Amour book be burned. Anyone who can inspire such malice from the elitist crowd is OK with me. L'Amour wrote very different types of novels than what she did and, of course, since she disagreed with him she wanted all his books burned. She also, no doubt, brags about her tolerance and compassion.

Western stories may be making a mild comeback these days. So any writer who wants to get on the Western bandwagon or stagecoach as the case may be should read L'Amour.

It could be said that L'Amour's heroes in one book are very much like his lead characters in other books and there is a degree of truth in that.

His men are typical Western laconic types. They are honest and honorable, competent, courageous and men of their word. They are not loquacious or neurotic or prone to panic. It's not accident that "Hondo" was written by L'Amour and played on the screen by John Wayne. He writes of the John Wayne, the Gary Coopers and the James Stewarts of history. His characters were based on real life. In his childhood, L'Amour talked to such men and listened as they told tales. Those tales enriched his own stories.

This is the man who said, "It is often said that one has but one life to live, but that is nonsense. For one who reads, there is no limit to the number of lives that may be lived, for fiction, biography and history offer an inexhaustible number of lives in many parts of the world, in all periods of time."

Very true.

The literary time of L'Amour was our American West and we were fortunate to have him in our midst.

While his stories were not all that complicated, they were textured and his characters fleshed out. His book "Shalako" was a sound Western but messed up by Hollywood. In one scene

European aristocrats have been taken captive by bandits. In the book, the aristocrats take a courageous stand, risking their lives. The bandits, even though they have all the guns, back down. It's a memorable scene. L'Amour did not have much patience with the rich, and the aristocratic follies, especially their arrogance, are on display the novel. But L'Amour knew this group of aristocrats were, in spite of all their flaws, brave. The scene gives them a depth and makes them three-dimensional human beings, not just stick figures. I won't tell you how badly the film screwed up this scene.

But the heroes of L'Amour time haven't passed from the world. I mentioned before the American soldiers who are now fighting with the Kurds against ISIS. I imagine they behave and talk very much like the men in L'Amour books. He makes them believable, fleshed-out human beings.

If you want to write about such heroes, it's a good idea to read a few books by this Medal of Freedom winner

Chapter 14:
Every Novel needs a Little Action

The major flaw in the prose of beginning writers, although every editor will tell you, is they tell instead of show. This is a killer for any novel. An author can't tell his story. He has to show it. So, how so you show instead of tell – action verbs.

Here is a brief exert from my novel "At Plays in the Seas of the Lord." (I would quote other authors extensively but that runs into copyright problems.)

"I dove left as the bullet zinged by and skimmed some bark off a tree. I fired as I hit the ground and heard a cry from behind the green bushes. I rolled as a second bullet whizzed over my head. A third slug thunked into the tree. When I fired again, another wail sounded. A man in dark clothes rose up and slapped a hand on his side. Blood flowed between his fingers and rolled down his pants. My next bullet put a second red hole in him as I heard the sickening smack of lead into belly flesh.

A Miami Dolphin tackle slammed into me and drove me to the ground."

I hope the reader get the point that there's a lot going on in this scene. The scene is about midway through the novel and, if the reader has stayed with me that long, I trust he will read this passage with avid interest. He obviously doesn't want the narrator to die. (I switched to the third person in parts of the book so it is possible the narrator won't be living at the end of the last chapter.)

But I trust you see the point with action verbs. You do not want to write a paragraph like this one

"I got up, got a cup of coffee and left the house. I picked up the paper and put it under my arm while walking. I walked two blocks then turned left and entered the restaurant and ordered breakfast. When the waitress brought it, I ate the eggs and bacon and skimmed through the paper. I found nothing interesting."

While there was nothing interesting in the paper there is nothing interesting in this paragraph either. If you string two or three paragraphs like this together your reader will soon look for another novel. A novel that has some action verbs and hopefully a good plot.

If you must have your narrator eat breakfast, there are better ways to do it such as.

"I poured a cup of coffee but it was black and tasted awful. Three minutes later I forked a piece of ham at a nearby restaurant. But I almost choked on the bacon when I saw the newspaper story."

Eating breakfast is a routine activity but you have caught the reader's interest.

Chapter 15

My friend and writing colleague, Gene Robinson, is a former professor at James Madison University. He was a member of the writing group I attended at Harrisonburg, Va. No he owns Moonshine Cove Publishing and, like all publishers, is looking for quality novels to publish.

He was kind enough to write this chapter to explain to new writers what he looks for in a manuscript and how he judges them.

WHAT WE LOOK FOR IN A QUERY LETTER AND MANUSCRIPT

Moonshine Cove Publishing, LLC (http://moonshinecovepublishing.com/) receives far more queries than we can publish. We therefore needed some method to help us separate the wheat from the chaff, so to speak. What we finally came up with is the method that has worked well for us over the past couple of years. We score each query letter using our Query Letter Evaluation Sheet consisting of eleven columns on a spread sheet. The first six columns are informational and mostly self-explanatory:

DATE

NAME

TITLE

WORDS

F - NF

GUIDELINES

The first five of these columns tells us what we most need to know about each author's query and potential manuscript submission. Nearly always we are pressed for time when we we're reading a query, so we want to get down to these basics as quickly as possible. That's why the Submissions page of our website, using a really large font, asks a basic question:

* Is the author's name, title of work, word count and genre listed at the top of the query?

That's the first thing we look for in the query. If we don't find it clearly shown at the top of the query, we have to skim down through the letter looking for this basic data. That wastes our time and puts us in a bad mood. You don't ever want to put someone in a bad mood who you are trying to convince to read your manuscript with the ultimate goal of getting a publishing contract. Some people never give all this information. That's bad, even worse than making us search for it. Why?

The first three should be obvious but what about the word count and whether it's fiction or non-fiction?

The word count is an important consideration to a publisher in deciding whether they're interested in a manuscript of not. For example, we just read a query for a novel a few minutes ago that listed 30,000 as the word count. That's too short to be a novel. It might be a great novella but we only publish novels so we're not interested. We've had others as short as 14,000— that's a short story, not a novel.

At the other end of the spectrum, if the word count gets much above about 115,000, we start to lose interest, unless the writing is really exceptional. There are good reasons for this. One factor is that more time is required at every stage of the book production process than a less wordy manuscript. Another is that it costs more money to produce the book and therefore, the book has to be priced higher, which hurts sales. The basic equation is whether we'd be better off producing two seventy-thousand word books than one that's twice as long. That answer almost always favors the two shorter books.

Is there a sweet spot for word count? Not really, but most of our books are 60 - 80,000 or so. When the count gets down to 50,000 we starting wondering if it isn't a bit light? Above 90,000, we starting to think the opposite.

For the F-NF column (fiction-nonfiction), we list the genre. There are some genres we like better than others and some we won't publish at all. Too many writers waste their time and ours by sending queries for genres we don't publish such as a fantasy novel.

Hint: Read our guidelines before sending a query.

What about the sixth column, Guidelines? Either a "Y" or "N" goes there. If it's an "N," the rest of your query and writing sample is going to have to be pretty darn special before we'll ask to see the full manuscript. Our reasoning is that if the writer couldn't follow these simple directions in writing something as important as a query, what are they going to be like to work with when the time comes to edit their manuscript? Part of our guidelines instruct the writer to paste the first five pages of the manuscript into the body of the email query. That's the writing sample, which we read before reading the query itself. If the writing sample stinks, we don't waste time reading the query.

So obviously for us, the writing sample is by far the most important part of the query, which brings us to the remaining five columns of our evaluation form:

5 pages?

Amazon

Comments

Verdict

Follow-Up

The "5 pages" column gets a number from 1 - 4, with one being as bad as bad can be and 4 being Hemingway Perfection. If you don't send the five pages as instructed, you get "None" written in this box. That pretty well guarantees you an "N" under Verdict, meaning we will not be asking for your manuscript and that you will eventually be receiving a politely worded rejection email.

Under "Comments," our write our impressions using cryptic phrases that help jog our memory when we go back over the sheet to look at those with "?" under Verdict. We put a "?" in the box if the query and writing sample isn't good enough to cause us to immediately ask for the manuscript, but, depending on the competition, we might at a later time. Yes, there's some luck to the process. If your 2½-quality writing sample lands next to a 3½, we might not ask for your manuscript that day, whereas at a later date, after reading a bunch of 1½s and 2s, we might ask for it. We try to reach a decision on all queries within two months and those with "?" get delayed the longest.

We will also note under "Comments" whether the writer has a realistic publicity-promotion-marketing plan and if so, how detailed it is. An original, well thought out marketing plan is certainly a plus in having us ask for the manuscript, but not a killer if the rest is good.

After we finish reading the five-page writing sample, we search the writer's name at Amazon to see if the writer has any books listed there, and if so, we check the publisher (Vanity Press or a real publisher?) and we check how well the book is selling. Having books published by a Vanity Press or Create Space, for us, does not count as being published.

Now let's look at how our scoring has worked in practice. Below is our spread sheet table, split into two sections to be legible on this page, with a few examples included.

DATE

NAME

TITLE

WORDS

F - NF

GUIDELINES

2/27

Laura Dempsey

Triple Cross

70k

F - crime

Y

1/10

Harris Mauldin

To Their Own God

106k

F - historical

N

3/17

Lucy Rosenthal

No Time to Cry

142k

F-romantic susp

N

2/18

Whitney Wells

Final Score

103k

F-sports

Y

5 pages?

Amazon

Comments

Verdict

Follow-Up

2½

Y - 1

Interesting; some minor writing errors (the usual) but we'd read more, already has 1 blurb

Y

Asked for MS 3/2

2½.

N

Pretty good; we'd keep reading; only 1 writing error but not our favorite era & no marketing

?

EMRJ 3/11

None

N

No 5 pages, no interest

N

EMRS 3/31

3

N

minor writing errors (barked as tag, 1 colon); good 5 pp, grabs interest; we'd read more.

Asked for MS 4/26

We'll discuss them in order beginning with the 2/27 query.

Laura followed the guidelines and the length is good. She has one published novel available at Amazon, but it's not a great seller. The writing sample is not super, but it's okay and it's interesting enough for us to keep reading. There are some minor writing errors but we consider it a plus that she realizes the importance of blurbs and already has one for her work. We emailed her right away for the manuscript.

Harris has an intriguing title and it's one of our favorite genres, historical fiction. It's long but not unusual for this genre, however, he didn't follow the guidelines, one strike. The writing sample is equal to Laura's, but we weren't interested in women pirates in the eighteenth century, or pirates in general for that matter. Combine that with nothing in the letter about promotion or marketing and we have strike two, but not yet a rejection, so we gave it a "?". We left it like that for two months until we went back and compared several other queries with "?"s under verdict. We picked the top one from the group and the others got our EMRS, shorthand for Email Rejection Sent.

Lucy also has a good title, but her work is really long for a romantic suspense novel. She didn't follow the guidelines and worst of all, she didn't submit the writing sample—another EMRS.

Whitney followed the guidelines and the work is long, but if it grabs our attention, that doesn't matter; and, this one did, with a score of "3." Not many receive that high a score (our highest ever is 3½). There are writing errors, including using body-language terms such as barked or growled as dialogue tags, instead of "said," which should be used most of the time. We see writers trying too hard with tags all the time, the most common writing error we see. Don't do it. There's also a colon. Colons are more appropriate for non-fiction than novels. It's okay to have a few colons in a novel, but if there's one in the first five pages, there are likely way too many in the manuscript. But, as so often happens, good writing overcomes a lot and we asked for the manuscript.

This system works for us, and now you know how to use it to your advantage. Send us a really "bang-up" writing sample in your query and the rest will probably take care of itself. There's really nothing new in this, however. We give pretty much the same information on our web page: http://moonshinecovepublishing.com/.

Our web page includes a contact form, but don't use it for queries. Instead send an email to:

publisher@moonshinecovepublishing.com

(I would add that, if you are looking for a publisher, I think Moonshine Cover is one of the finest around. I have sent a few queries letters to agents and publishers and, when the reply came back, I doubted they had even been read. When I sent a query about my latest novel "Last Stand at Lighthouse Point," the reply stated the company didn't do children's books. Well, "Lighthouse" is anything but a children's book. Oh, well.

As you see from this chapter, a mistake of that magnitude would never be made by Moonshine Cove. Gene runs an excellent, ethical company. If you're looking for a publisher....

Chapter 16:
Structure, Editing

Sir, you said you would discuss structure and editing in this chapter but isn't structure and your plot the same thing?

Not really, Diane, although at times the words have been used interchangeably. Plot is your theme and all that goes on in your novel. Structure is more how you tell the story. First person, Second person. Fifth person."

Fifth person? You're putting us on, right sir?

Yes, just wanted to make sure you're paying attention. There is no fifth person. But your literary structure might employ say, an unreliable narrator, or have a very, multi-layered plot. However, as beginning writers I would advise against. First, I've never liked novels with unreliable narrators. That's very difficult to pull off in a realistic manner. And until you get more experience in writing and plots, I suggest just the basic bare bones plot is the best for the first one or two novels. The first person narrative is the easiest for the beginning writer, which is why so many use it. But it is limiting. You are limited to what the narrator sees, says, does or thinks. A third person narrative allows for a richer novel. Experience novels will experiment with different narratives and even combine a few. But, again, it's best try first or third person narrative until you get more experience.

Did I hear you say, sir, that editing is the bane of a writer's existence?

Yes, you did Diane. The Indie market has allowed many writers to published their own works, which is a good thing. A would-be writer doesn't have to go through the gatekeepers of the publishing industry. It has also allowed a number of entrepreneurial men and women to open their own publishing company and start scanning for quality novels. There are a few critics of this process. They claim that 95 percent of Indie publishing offering will be trash. Which is probably true. But it's also true that 95 percent of major publishers are trash. Any number of incredibly bad writers have, in the past, been printed by major publishers. Besides there is Sturgeon's Law. It states that 90 percent of anything is mediocre. (And I cleaned that up a bit. The original saying did not use the word mediocre.)

But there is one clear advantage the larger publishers have on the small, independent ones Can you guess what that is class?

More copy editors, sir?

Exactly. When I was in journalism there was a saying You should never read your own work." That's true. You will miss errors, typos, etc. What was true in journalism is also true in writing novels. It's difficult reading your own work. You need a second set of eyes. This is why there is often more typos and mistakes, sometimes a great many more, in Indie publishing than a novel from a mainstream press.

This is really annoying to the reader. He would like an error-free book. As would the author, of course. Which is easier said than done. Most Indie publishers do not have two or three copy editors on hand.

If are publishing outside the mainstream, see if you can get one or two friends, hopefully English majors, to copy read your novel before it's published. I did have a friend look over "Last Stand at Lighthouse Point" and she did find a number of errors I had missed.

 There are editors available on such sites as e-lance that will copy editor your novel and also do developmental editing. The bids are competitive and you can get a good price.

I do freelance writing and have taken on e-lance jobs. One client recently wrote me say "our novel" was accepted by a publisher and is now on

Amazon and other outlets. I'm very happy for him. If you seek an editor on e-lance you will have to weed through the applicants but you should be able to find a highly qualified editor to help with your needs at a relative low price. Also, if you find a good editor, then by all mean use him or her for your next novel too.

If the developmental editor suggests changes and we disagree, what do we do, sir?

Stay with your own judgment. It's your novel. It's your vision. There may be suggestions that you can willingly accept. I revised by client's outline of his novel on several occasions. Thankfully, he agreed with my modifications. I think my revisions allowed the novel to flow better and made it more rational and scientific. (It was a science fiction novel but I think the changes made the fiction more solidly based on science.) Anyway, he liked and e-mailed me that two publishers were interested in it.

If you agree with any modifications, fine. If not, then reject them. Good editors are not there to mandate changes, just to make suggestions.

Sir, not that I'm complaining but it seems that if writers go the Indie route, they will have to be more than writers. They will have to be editors, copy editors, marketers, business people, etc.

Yes, Diane you are right. But, for the most part, writers have always needed to market their books. In the past major publishers did major marketing for their major writers. Other, lesser-known writers were more likely on their own. But, let's face it, writing is a business and the writer at times has to be a rapacious marketer if he wants his business to succeed. However, word-of-mouth, particularly in a high-tech age is very important. If you get a few readers and they praise your novel on Fackebook, Twitter and every other form of social media, it can get sales rolling.

Not me. I'm seventy-nine years old.

"Yes, Mr. Arnold. You might be lacking in social media skills. But ask your grandchildren to help you. They will probably know a great deal about social media and can help you turn your novel into a best seller. That also goes for the all the members of the class who are over fifty. If you don't have grandkids, then Diane will help you.

Yes, I certainly will. Just give me a call.

Thank you, Diane. All my best, class.

In Conclusion

Every beginning writer wants to be published. And every beginning writer generally wants to continue being published. But at the start of a career sometimes getting published appears to be daunting.

But there is one trait that, if used consistently, will probably guarantee that you will get published. If this trait is used daily or at least five out of the seven days of the week, I'm guessing there's a 95 percent chance you will get your novel eventually in print.

No, it's not talent. (Although talent is a very good trait to have.)

It's discipline.

It's going to the computer every day or six days out of the week, sitting down and typing out a chapter. It's setting a quota of about 1,000 words a day and hitting that goal Monday through Saturday. (Although if you're having one of those days when writing seems as tough as slogging your way through a Amazon rain forest with a machete, do 990 words and take the afternoon off.)

You will need persistence and discipline.

After spending the war in the China-Burma-India region, John D. MacDonald began his writing career. He papered his wall with rejection slips. (They came in the mail back in those days.) That's right. He papered the wall with them. You can imagine how many he got.

He did not quit.

He persevered.

And became one of the finest writers in the 20th century. Chances are he will still be read fifty years from now and, I'm guessing, a hundred years from now.

Even if you don't like mysteries, anyone reading one of MacDonald's Travis McGee mysteries will get a slice of life of south Florida circa 1962-88. You probably didn't think simply describing where you live would provide literary immortality but it might. It does help MacDonald gives you Florida in all its tainted beauty wrapped up in a excellent mystery.

But the point is MacDonald didn't quit. He came from a business background and perhaps that helped. Screw creativity. He had a job to do and he went into his office, sat down at his typewriter and did it. For a long time no one cared what he was writing. A lesser man would have given up and gone back into the business world.

But he persisted.

Slowly, the rejection slips became acceptance slips. One by one, the mystery magazines became to recognize this newcomer. After he sold numerous short stories he began writing novels. And probably toiled for almost twenty years before finally hitting the best seller list.

For during the months and possibly years of getting nothing published, he was learning about plot, dialogue, pace, setting, etc. Those days of getting nothing but rejection slips were not wasted.

I remember two items about two very different science fiction writers, Norman Spinrad and Larry Niven. Niven writes what is called "hard science fiction" and Spinrad writes anything but. But I recall reading that it took both of them about a year of full-time writing before they made a sale.

That's a year. For two SF writers who are among the best in the field.

To be honest, if Niven or Spinrad didn't get a sale before a year's time spent at the keyboard, you shouldn't expect a sale within three months after you start.

But they did not quit and neither should you.

Many SF fans and critics consider "Dune" the finest science fiction novel every written. If I recall, it was rejected by more than two dozen publishers. Since Dune is a rather large book, author Frank Herbert must have been a bit depressed that all the time and effort he spent on the book might be for nothing. But a publisher finally did accept it and history was made.

I'm guessing that halfway through this epic novel Herbert wondered if it would sell or if he was wasting his time. All humans have doubts occasionally.

But Herbert persisted.

And produced the best science fiction novel ever written.

Persistence is probably more important than talent. There are any number of published writers – and well selling published writers – who have very little talent.

But they persevered.

If you will too, no matter the odds, there's a very good chance that one day you will see a novel with your name on it.